A new hypersonic plane called Fireflash was getting ready to fly from London to Australia. All the passengers were excited to be on such an amazing plane!

Kayo wished she could fly alone on Thunderbird Shadow. "It's a shame Thunderbird Shadow's being repaired," she told Scott.

Then, soon after Fireflash took off, a strange thing happened. The plane vanished from the radar! The air controller at the airport called International Rescue for help.

"The plane hasn't crashed," John said, "but I can't see it either!"

John told the others about the problem. Scott was puzzled.

"I spoke to Kayo just now," he said. "Everything was fine."

Up in the sky, the captain told the passengers to put on their oxygen masks. Moments later, everyone was fast asleep – except Kayo.

"This is strange," she thought. "Something's going on!"

Kayo kept quiet. When it was safe, she slipped into the cockpit of the plane.

The co-pilot was asleep, and Kayo couldn't wake him. "Hmm …" she thought. "The co-pilot's out cold. This isn't exactly normal! The captain must be up to no good."

Then Kayo noticed something strange under the control panel. It was a cloaking device: a machine to stop the plane appearing on radar!

Kayo ripped away the cloaking device. Suddenly, the plane was back on radar.

Kayo wondered who the captain was. She peeped through the door and ran a face check.

"Oh no!" she gasped. "It's The Hood, International Rescue's old enemy! He's in disguise!"

"International Rescue, I need your help!" said Kayo. "The Hood has hijacked Fireflash!"

Scott climbed into Thunderbird 1 to catch up with Fireflash. Virgil, Alan and Gordon followed in Thunderbird 2.

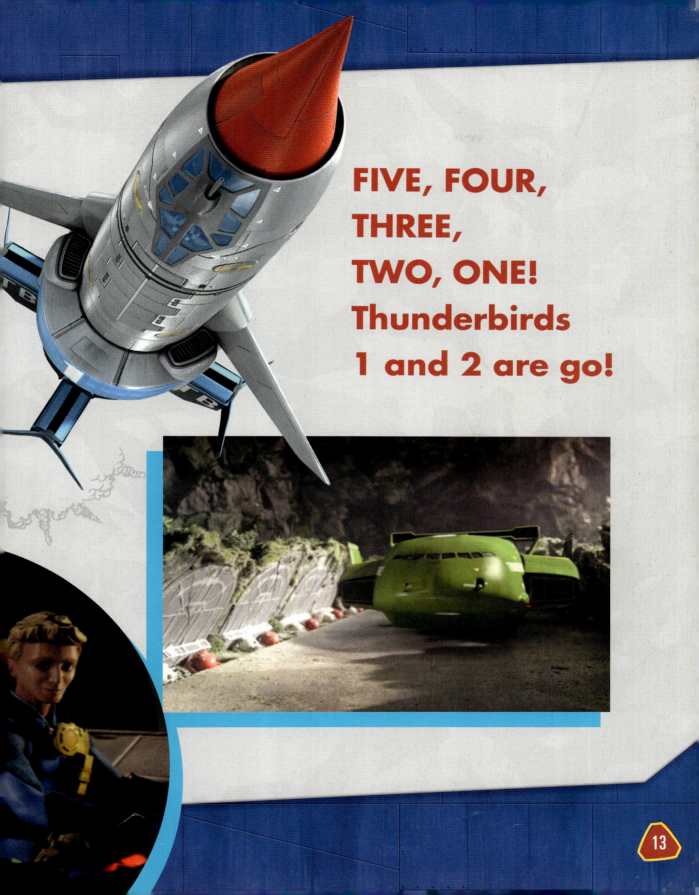

**FIVE, FOUR, THREE, TWO, ONE!** Thunderbirds 1 and 2 are go!

When The Hood spotted that his cloaking device had gone, he went to look for the person who had taken it.

Kayo was hiding in the luggage area of Fireflash.

The Hood went down into the luggage area. "I know you're hiding in here!" he called.

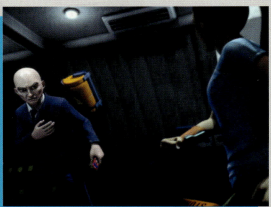

When The Hood found Kayo, she stood up to him bravely.

He smashed one of the plane's fuel tanks, and fuel started to leak into the luggage area.

Quickly, The Hood climbed into an escape POD. He thought the leaking fuel would make the plane blow up, so he wanted to get away.

"Good luck landing this plane!" he said to Kayo, as he zoomed off in the POD.

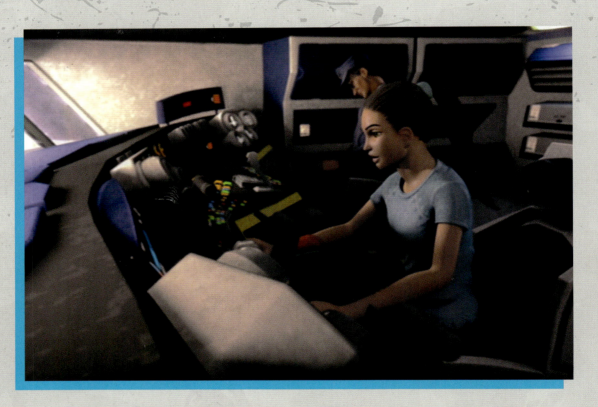

Kayo was worried. The plane had no pilot now! She had to land it herself, before the fuel could catch fire.

Kayo called Scott in Thunderbird 1.
"It's OK," he told her. "Thunderbird 2's pods will help you land safely!"

Kayo started to get Fireflash ready to land, but only one of its wheels came down.

"You can't land like that – the plane will fall apart!" said Scott.

Gordon and Alan climbed into Thunderbird 2's PODs and were soon on the runway. They raised their landing pads for Kayo.

This plan didn't work either. "The plane's too heavy! It's crushing us!" cried Gordon.

Kayo lifted the plane off the PODs.

"I'm out of fuel!" she gasped.
"Things look very bad –
the plane could crash!"

Then Virgil used Thunderbird 2's cables to catch Fireflash. He gently put the plane on the runway. At last, they were safe.

"Well done, Kayo," said Scott. "All the passengers on Fireflash owe their lives to you!"

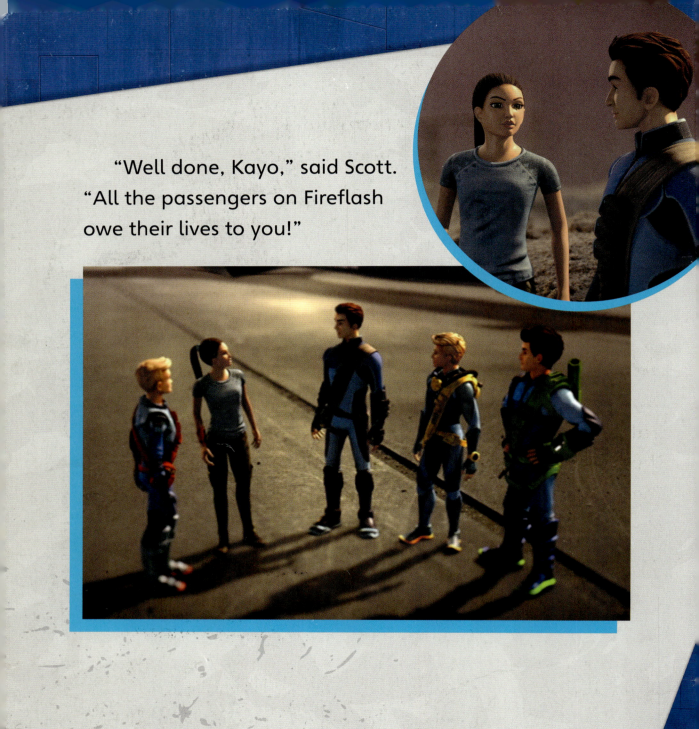